Life Links

Four Friends. Seven Relationships. One God.

ROBIN R. SMITH

Life Links
Four Friends. Seven Relationships. One God.

Published by MLStimpson Enterprises
P.O. Box 1592, Cedar Hill, TX 75106
ISBN 978-1-943563-33-3

Cover design by Robin R. Smith and Michelle Stimpson.

Editing by Tonia Robertson.

DEDICATION

To real women, living real lives, in relationships with real people, depending on the one true God, Who is absolutely real.

CONTENTS

CONTENTS

APPLAUSE FOR *LIFE LINKS*

If you don't know Robin Smith, this is your chance to get to know her. *Life Links* is a beautiful book. The narratives are cinematic in scope, and reading it feels like enjoying a quiet conversation with an old friend. Don't miss this opportunity to celebrate storytelling at its best. *Life Links* is rooted in biblical truths and speaks to the diversity of women's lives in these four imminently relatable and altogether unforgettable protagonists. This work encourages, edifies, and like any great read, leaves you savoring the experience and wishing for more. Get ready, get set, read!

Marilyn Randle, Co-Author
Coveted Conversations
The Image Bearer
Tabletop Conversations

APPLAUSE FOR *LIFE LINKS*

Life Links captures the complexities and triumphs of women of color. Recognizing the influences of African American women – family, childhood friendships, and church life – the relationships in this book tell how they mold and meld our personalities as well as our character. The intriguing questions allow us to reflect and possibly rethink matters from a different perspective. As each of the four friends grows in age and maturity, they learn more about themselves and resist the ever-present struggle to be accepted by others. We can all learn from their persistence.

Vanessa F. Hardeman, Home Educator

ACKNOWLEDGMENTS

To my indescribable and inexplicable God, Who is above all, and through all, and in us all, and Who is ever faithful. Thank You, Lord!

To my husband of 30 years, David. Thank you for your unwavering love, for always supporting who I am, and for celebrating who God created me to be.

To my mother, Mrs. Mary L. Hatcher, who for as far back as my memory will carry me, taught me to always use my voice and make my case. Thank you for showing me how to live my life as a lady of confidence and class.

To my editor, Tonia Robertson. Thank you for your expertise, and for your willingness to support my work.

And to my publisher, Michelle Stimpson. Your guidance and contributions have allowed me to bring this story to life.

FOREWORD

It is an honor to pen the foreword for this exciting book on relationships. Relationships are so powerful in that they can determine our destiny. They are multifaceted and can be complicated. As we relate to others, we can't control their perception of us, but we *are* responsible for what we convey to them, through our attitudes, and through our character, or lack thereof.

In *Life Links*, you will get to know each of these four women intimately as you explore how they navigate different relationships.

I have had the privilege of authoring a book on marital relationships. I was married to my husband Vernon for 48 years before his passing in 2018. In addition, I have spent the last 30 years speaking to millions of people across the United

States, Europe, Asia, and Australia. Everywhere I travel in this world, I realize one thing: God created us to be relational. The cultures may be different, but the need for healthy relationships is the same.

First, we need to have an authentic relationship with God. Second, we need to have meaningful relationships with one another. And finally, we need to be honest when relating to our true selves. In her book *Life Links*, my sister and friend Robin has done an exceptional job in the way she has communicated the various dynamics of relationships, and how we can manage them in healthy ways.

Robin is a remarkable woman, and she is a creative storyteller. She loves people with a real passion, and she has the ability to embrace people wherever they are, without compromising her own Godly principles. She is a safe place for people to come and find acceptance, absent of judgment. She is committed to loving her friends unconditionally, and she brings a wealth of knowledge to this book by way of her own experiences. Robin truly wants the very best for people, and she is always excited to celebrate others.

None of us is perfect; we are all in the process of growing. For this reason, it is Robin's desire that we learn to accept ourselves, become comfortable in who we are, and be transparent in our relationships, never excusing sinful behavior, but always striving to have a heart that pleases God.

Life Links is a great read. It will grab your attention, it will make you think, and it will cause you to examine your relationships.

Enjoy!

Dr. Patricia Ashley, Conference Speaker
Author, Marriage is a Blessing

PREFACE

Four girls meet as students at Elevated Education Academy, an all-girls' school in Chicago. They each choose to enroll in an elective class, *Local Multiculturalism*, taught by Mrs. Sheila Langow. Being a part of this class has unearthed thoughts and opinions each girl was unaware she even had. Opening up and sharing their viewpoints sparks an undeniable connection, which leads them to form a remarkable friendship.

This story chronicles the first decade of their lives following high school graduation as they begin to grow into lovely, intelligent young women. Coming into adulthood takes them onto some mountaintops high and through some valleys low, and they learn many lessons along the way. They learn about relationships. They learn about their true selves. They learn about God. They learn about *life*.

After being introduced to Onyx, to Candace, to Lorraine, and to Amber, as you continue reading, you will get to know each of them even better. *Life Links* gives you a front row seat and an in-depth look at their lives, exploring each girl's relationship with her mother, with her father, with her best friend, with dating and marriage, with her church family, with herself, and with her God.

How are mother-daughter relationships formed? What factors into how fathers and daughters relate? Are there differences in either or both relationships if the parents were never married or if they divorce? What constitutes a best friend? What shapes our views on dating? On marriage? On our choice of whether or not to marry? Why do we choose to become part of a certain church? What, if anything, draws us to that group? What causes us to remain with a particular congregation, perhaps for decades? What do we really think about ourselves, at the core of our being? What do we think about God? What do we think about what He, in His Sovereignty, allows into our lives?

These four friends asked themselves some of these same questions, and maybe after spending some time with each of them, you will look within to find answers of your own.

MEET

Onyx Alexander

❦

Onyx Alexander. A tall, thin, chocolate girl with a beautiful head of long, straight, shiny, hip-length black hair. Like the mane on a horse's back. Onyx's hair flowed and followed after her as she walked, as she took each thought-through step. It was full and luxurious, like they describe in the shampoo commercials.

Not to throw shade, but Onyx's hair was scalp hair. It was not horse's hair, no pun intended. Not that there is anything wrong with that. She just wanted it to be on the record. Onyx was a fierce proponent of a girl doing all she could to enhance her beauty, and to make herself feel good about how she looks. She believed if you want it, and you can't grow it, why *not* buy it? Put it on, pin it down, and get on with your life, feeling fabulous all the way.

Onyx knew how to walk. Like those runway models who sport that pony walk. Every pickup and put down of each foot had a purpose. And to revisit the hair conversation, if hair could talk, hers absolutely made a statement. She had her Mama Lynn to thank for those tresses. Onyx's parents were African American, but her Mama Lynn, her great-grandmother on her mother's side, was full Cherokee Indian. It took three generations, but Ms. Octavia was thrilled about her daughter's head of hair, especially since Onyx barely had peach fuzz until she was a little over a year old.

Just like the girl in the Song of Solomon, Onyx was dark and lovely. And she was delighted to be. She was an elegant, classy girl, working in the finance industry as an investment broker. She could hold her own with any counterpart, regardless of gender or generation, ethnicity or experience. She stayed on the ready, and recognition from peers and superiors alike, along with her numerous workplace awards, was living proof.

In the course of her work, was Onyx ever offered information prior to it being made public? She was. Was she tempted to make some questionable deals here and there? She was. Everybody did it. That was the nature of the business. If she were a man, not only would it have been tolerated, it would have been accepted, and even expected. But she chose to do the job for which she was hired without compromising who she was. That is why she was respected. And that is why she was crushing it in the company.

ONYX AND HER MOM, MS. OCTAVIA

Onyx and her mom had a great relationship. Ms. Octavia had always encouraged her daughter to openly communicate with her, to broach any subject she had questions about. Her reasoning was simple. She knew Onyx was on her way to where she had already been, and if Onyx took heed to the pearls of wisdom her mother shared, she could save herself a lot of heartache.

Ms. Octavia was a very wise woman. She believed being wise meant applying spiritual truths to life's realities. But even more than that, she knew the fear of the Lord is the beginning of wisdom. Hearing her mom's voice could sometimes be akin to Onyx reading her own bible, because much of what came from Ms. Octavia's lips was straight scripture.

Ms. Octavia had lots of favorite bible verses, some of

which were mandatory that Onyx commit to memory. She knew from experience the value of hiding the Word in one's heart, and she passed that on to her children. Through the various stages of maturity, from early childhood, through adolescence, her teenage years, and into young adulthood, one scripture remained in the forefront of Onyx's mind:

Bad company corrupts good character.
I Corinthians 15:33

Ms. Octavia began reading that scripture to Onyx at a very early age. Onyx asked, as any curious child would, "What is bad company?" "What is corrupt?" "What is character?" Ms. Octavia answered every question, explaining each word along the way. It wasn't until she was confronted with a fourth-grade situation that Onyx truly understood the worth of that scripture.

It was the first day of school, and at lunchtime, Onyx met two new students, Darsi and Nyla. The three of them seemed to hit it off. They had fun hanging out together. But Nyla started to get into fights, which led to her spending less time in the classroom and more time in the principal's office.

Just as Onyx started to wonder whether she should distance herself from Nyla, she learned Nyla was only getting into trouble because she had been egged on by Darsi, to make a name for herself as a tough girl. And Nyla was all too happy to oblige. Immediately, a light went off in Onyx's head. She was grateful for a mother who taught her about character, and who was the embodiment of Proverbs 31:26:

She speaks with wisdom, and faithful instruction is on her tongue.

And Onyx was even more grateful that this wise woman was faithful to pass that instruction on to her daughter.

ONYX AND HER DAD, MR. LINCOLN

*O*nyx's dad was a pharmaceutical salesman, and he was a natural. Mr. Lincoln could sell bacon to a pig. He could get anyone to buy anything. Whether or not they needed it or wanted it was irrelevant. He had the charm. He had the smooth. And he could be very persuasive. Just ask Ms. Octavia. To this day, she wonders if she fell in love with Mr. Lincoln or if he just convinced her to buy what he was selling: a promise of a lifetime of love and adventure. The one thing she could never dispute is that he hadn't disappointed her.

For the first 15 years of their marriage, Mr. Lincoln was seldom home. His job required him to be on the road three out of four weeks of every month. He really *was* a traveling salesman. He didn't like having to spend so much time away from his wife and children, but he enjoyed what he did, and he was very good at it. His schedule would finally relax some, and Ms. Octavia was happy to have him home a whole lot more.

It would be nearly 35 years before Mr. Lincoln would retire from Meltrane Medical, and Onyx resented just about every one of those years. He tried to explain why he hadn't been around as much when she was younger. He needed her to understand that he wanted the best for his family, and that required him to be away. He wanted her and her brothers to grow up in a nice house with a big yard. He wanted his children to go to the best private schools. He wanted his family to live in a safe neighborhood, because the last thing he needed was to worry about their well-being. But those "wants" had price tags attached, and those price tags required him to earn an above-average salary. Way above.

But none of that mattered to Onyx. All she knew was that she missed her dad. She enjoyed the things he provided, and she appreciated his sacrifice. Still, from the time she was a little girl, she just wanted to have breakfast with her dad in the morning and hug him before she went to bed at night. Now that she was older, she realized she should be grateful to have him home with her now. And she was.

ONYX AND HER BESTIE, TORREY

*O*nyx and Torrey both loved old school R&B music, and they each heard it often in their homes growing up. Everybody from Aretha Franklin and The Pointer Sisters to Sam Cooke and Earth, Wind & Fire. And they could sing along to all the lyrics of all their hit songs.

During their third year of college as wide-eyed professionals-to-be, Onyx and Torrey knew where they'd be nearly every Friday night. Just after the Fall semester began, a poetry café opened in what was the College Community Court, just north of the school grounds. Triple C, as the students called it, was an area for students to shop and socialize without having to go far from school property. The girls had seen the flyers advertising *Talented Talk* posted around campus, but they didn't start hanging out there until word got out that it was *the* place to be. And of course, they loved the fact that there was always an old school R&B musical backdrop to the poets' orations.

Mrs. J. H. Rydington, an affluent alumnus of Shambrough Intercontinental College, donated funds to the city to construct Triple C. She had fond memories of her time on that campus, but she also remembered some of the not-so-wise decisions made by some of her fellow classmates. Unfortunately, Mrs. Rydington knew all too well that young people didn't always think things through. So, in the interest of encouraging better choices, and to somehow atone for a deadly choice her son had made, she gave her resources to provide a space for current and future students to responsibly enjoy the social side of their collegiate lives.

Mrs. Rydington's son Hudson had been convicted of intoxication manslaughter. The Rydingtons had the means to make the problem go away, but she and her late husband James vowed they would never be the kinds of well-to-do parents who made difficulties disappear to cover mistakes or to preserve their family's good name. They believed everyone should be held accountable for his or her actions, and that is how they raised Hudson. And Hudson had no delusions about how his mother would respond to his careless actions. He had known from the time he was a toddler, what his parents said, they meant.

Mrs. Rydington knew there was nothing she could do to give her son's victim his life back, but she had to do something. She felt her gift of Triple C gave the parents of students at her alma mater one less thing to worry about.

She also insisted a shuttle service be a part of the Triple C project. She knew young people enjoyed evenings out, dining and dancing with friends. She wanted to ensure they had no need to get behind the wheel of a car after having had a glass of wine. They could simply board the shuttle for the 20-minute commute back to campus.

Onyx and Torrey appreciated Mrs. R, and they made it their mission to urge the entire student body to take advantage of what their school had been given. Besides, these girls wanted to be known for being smart *and* being sensible.

ONYX AND HER GUY, GREG

Onyx had been promoted to VP and was now working exclusively with high-profile clients. Greg Garrison had just renewed his contract as a center with the Salem Ballers, a five-year deal reportedly worth $98M. Greg had spoken with Nathan Daniels, Asset Assurance Investment's CEO, informing him of his desire to have the best on staff in charge of his accounts. He said the brotha needed to be outstanding. When Nathan saw Greg's portfolio, he knew exactly who that person should be.

Onyx was running late, but even as she hurried into her office, she couldn't help but notice this unusually tall man headed toward the conference room with Nathan. She knew this guy had to be important to have scored a face-to-face with Nathan.

There were other staffers currently available to meet with Greg, but after getting a text from Onyx that she was a little behind schedule, Nathan asked Greg if he wouldn't mind waiting a few minutes. He was going to be sure this client got nothing less than the best broker at AAI. Nathan made a mental note of Greg's remark that the 'brotha' needed to be outstanding, but he said nothing. He knew as soon as Greg laid eyes on Onyx, he would know the top broker at AAI was definitely *not* a brotha, and five minutes into the meeting, he would know she was indeed outstanding. In fact, she was inarguably the best investment broker in the company.

After agreeing to move a little more than 70% of his investments to AAI, Greg was very impressed with the choices Onyx was making. She worked hard and she worked smart. She studied charts and graphs relentlessly, and she knew exactly when to buy and sell shares to yield the best return for her clients. Greg found that alluring, her being a powerful woman. So he went for it. He asked her out. He figured since she knew so much about him, and about his money, he might as well get to know her too.

Onyx enjoyed Greg's company, and she was a basketball fan, so the perk of free tickets didn't hurt. They saw each other whenever he was in town for home games, and sometimes when he wasn't scheduled to be. He was smitten with Onyx, so it was worth catching the red eye to see her, and then catching another one less than 24 hours later to make sure he made team curfew.

After being swept off her feet and a whirlwind romance

of less than eight months, Onyx became Mrs. Gregory Graham Garrison, III. They knew Greg would be on the road a lot, four to five months of the year. And Onyx was already working 50 to 60 hours every week. But they rationalized it. Since he was away, and she was working crazy long hours, it wouldn't be a problem. And it wasn't a problem. Until it was.

Onyx and Greg were each financially stable and doing very well as single people. Before they met, she had a solid career in finance, and he had long since made his mark in the NBA. Needless to say, on any list of problems, money was never one of them. But there were other issues. They liked each other and they loved each other. They just had very different ideas of what marriage was, and about what roles they each should play.

Greg had been raised to think a certain way about men and women, about husbands and wives, and about how they should relate. And he wasn't willing to change his views. He had tired of the time and distance between them. He wanted Onyx to be wherever he was, and he expected her to acquiesce. And she missed him too, but she didn't want to give up her job. She didn't *have* to work, but she *wanted* to work. She felt disrespected by his assumption that she would upend her career just to be at his disposal.

Greg began finding reasons to stay away longer for road games. When Onyx shared her feelings about him spending even more time away, Greg would justify it by telling her she had no problem with him being away before. He would taunt her by saying his being away was what primarily funded their plush lifestyle. He would brush her words aside and say to her, "My being away enables you to shop at Saks and wear Christian Louboutin and drive that Jag in the garage." She would snap back with, "I was shopping and wearing and driving when I met you!" Greg's words were painful reminders of her childhood, of how her dad would defend being away so that he could give them things. Having those feelings bubble up again nearly made her nauseas.

It became apparent where this relationship was heading. Downhill. And fast. Greg started spending even more time away. Even when he was home, he was still away from home. Onyx had always been a bit of a workaholic, so now, rather than come home to an empty house, she would just stay at the office. After several months, Onyx and Greg agreed to end their marriage. They didn't hate each other, they just no longer wanted to be a couple.

The divorce was amicable. Greg wasn't a bad person, he was just unyielding. He still loved Onyx and she still loved him. And he had plenty of bank, so he had no problem being generous with her in the settlement. He gave her the one thing he could, financial security, further pressing his assertion that she didn't have to work.

Greg had played with teammates who, when their marriages failed, hid money out of a need to punish their exes for the sake of humiliation. But Greg saw no need for any of that, neither by underreporting income nor concealing assets. Besides, Onyx had been Greg's financial advisor for the past seven years. She was privy to the bulk of his true net worth, not just what was reported in the media. She knew what the real numbers were.

They didn't part as friends. Instead, they remained friends, proud that they were quite mature for two twenty-somethings.

ONYX AND HER CHURCH,
GREATER ST. LUKE BAPTIST CHURCH

astor Wilson announced Greater St. Luke would host the city-wide women's conference this year. Churches of all sizes were invited to participate, from memberships of 200 to 20,000. This year would be special because it was the conference's 25th anniversary.

The conference theme was *To Speak or Not To Speak: That is the Question.* The keynote speaker was Sis. Kamille Vanton. Onyx knew Sis. Vanton very well. She had spent many evenings at the Vanton Family dinner table, with her bestie. Ms. Kamille was Torrey's mom, and for Onyx, being in the Vanton house was just like being at home.

Ms. Octavia and Ms. Kamille raised their girls with God-centered values. They were the kinds of mothers who were straightforward and did not play. And neither of them was the least bit concerned as to whether their mothering style was popular.

Ms. Kamille used hints of humor and loads of transparency when she spoke at conferences. That, along with her ability to relate to all kinds of women, her "sista-girls" as she called them, kept her calendar filled with speaking engagements.

After an anointed time of praise and worship, Ms. Kamille opened by reciting the conference title, and then asking for a show of hands in answer to her question. "Who likes to talk a lot?", she asked. About two-thirds of the group's hands went up. She then proposed that the lesser faction, the ladies who had not raised their hands, was the wiser, advocating that people who weren't always talking just might be a little more insightful. They certainly were more prudent, she suggested. That group knew you learned much more simply by listening.

She went on to explain that talking is overrated. She admonished the ladies to speak only when necessary. And when you *do* speak, she said, when you *do* share your viewpoint, remember that *how* you say what you say is just as important as what you say. She told the attendees her grandmother would often say "you get more flies with honey than with vinegar". Until Onyx was old enough to understand what that maxim meant, she thought to herself, *Who wants flies? We always shooed them away or swatted them.* But now she got it. People are more receptive to what you have to say if you say it with a smile in your voice.

"Eight of the 33 verses in Proverbs 15 give us great insight into speaking to each other", she continued, "especially verse 23":

A person finds joy in giving an apt reply—
and how good is a timely word!

She reminded the ladies that unless you are offering a word of encouragement to your sister, you would be wise to open your mouth to God, but not to her. You really don't need to *always* have something to say. It may not be time to speak. She expressed to the group that the tug you may feel to say something, that gut feeling, may instead be the Spirit of the Lord speaking to your inner self. "Tell her to listen", she said, "and to obey". To speak or not to speak? The answer, for right now, Ms. Kamille said, just may be no.

When she had finished speaking, Onyx and Torrey knew that beyond straight-up truth, Ms. Kamille had served up a hefty dose of practical application sprinkled with a little bit of wittiness. And so had the 3,500 ladies who had descended upon Greater St. Luke's campus that day.

ONYX AND HER INNER WOMAN

here was a time when many African American girls wished they were "bright", meaning light-skinned, and that they had what was deemed as "good hair", which meant it was naturally longer, wonderfully wavy, and always manageable. But Onyx always embraced her deep brown skin. It was how she came to acquire the nickname "Choco" (pronounced chock-oh), short for chocolate.

It was inevitable that at every family reunion, she would hear relatives say she had her father's color, as well as his killer smile. And since hair is now a bona fide accessory, changed from day to day like designer shoes and handbags, the length, color, and style of hair have become a matter of whatever mood you happen to wake up in. It really *is* no longer that serious.

Onyx knew she was gifted, but she also knew that any

good thoughts or deeds or possessions she had were given to her directly from the Hand of God. She had an infectious presence and an almost celebrity influence. She also had an enormous amount of power, not only in her company, but in the financial industry at large. People made fortunes based on her valuations. People whose incomes far exceeded upper middle class, by anyone's standards.

As anyone in any leadership position can attest to, power can be intoxicating. Power can cause you to think more highly of yourself than you ought to. Onyx had long since received the warning given in Romans 12:3:

Do not think of yourself more highly than you ought,
but rather think of yourself with sober judgment,
in accordance with the faith God has distributed to each of you.

Onyx had been given much power, and therefore, much more would be required of her because she had it.

Being integrous in every interaction with every person on every occasion was of utmost importance to her. To that end, she made sure she kept herself in check. Whenever pride tried to rear its ugly head, she remembered if she followed pride anywhere, it would only lead her to destruction. And if she allowed pride to puff her up, she would become so full of herself that she would indeed topple over, and she would indeed fall. She was committed to doing everything in her "power" to make sure that didn't happen.

ONYX AND GOD HER HELPER

*O*nyx was grateful for the life she was living. She was grateful for the many advantages that being financially solvent afforded her. She knew what a great blessing that was. But she wanted to make sure no one got it twisted. She would say openly to all who would listen that she knew, apart from God, she couldn't do a thing. She knew where her help came from, and she knew God was her Helper.

Riches were not anything Onyx ever prayed for, or even wanted. Yes, she wanted to live comfortably, not through any sense of entitlement, nor through anyone giving her anything. She was advised by her parents to dream big and to work hard to see those dreams fulfilled. She wanted to make her parents proud. She wanted to be able to take care of herself, and when the time came, to take care of them. And to share with those in need. She was cash comfortable, but she placed no confidence in that. Onyx knew finances were a resource. God is, and always would be, the Source.

Onyx needed help to get her through the divorce. She needed help keeping her feet firmly planted on the ground. She needed help to continue to be effective in her career. And in those hours when it was just her and her, when she was having deep and deliberate conversations with herself, when she was alone with her thoughts, she needed God's help. She was thankful to have that help manifested in the form of the unseen Hand of God, holding her up with His Righteous Right Hand.

Onyx had learned that help is support. Help requires the person to have an active part. Help is not doing it, help is coming alongside and assisting you *as you do it*. She'd heard it said *God helps those who help themselves*. And that was countered with, *If that's true, then who helps the helpless?* Onyx didn't believe in helplessness. One, she knew God had always promised to be her Helper, therefore, she could never truly be helpless. She knew He would providentially arrange circumstances that placed help in her path. And two, she would always have a part to play. She believed God gives her freedom of choice. And He's so amazing that His Word, in Deuteronomy 30:19-20, counsels her in that choice. He directs her to choose life!

This day I call the heavens and the earth as witnesses against
you that I have set before you life and death, blessings and
curses. Now choose life, so that you and your children may live

and that you may love the LORD your God, listen to his voice,
and hold fast to him. ...For the LORD is your life.

Her active part is to choose. He helps her by giving her the freedom to choose, and then again, by recommending what He knows is the best choice.

When you are young, gifted, and black, you might be tempted to think help is something you don't really need. Especially when you're young. Young people tend to lean toward invincibility. They rarely ask for or think they need help. From conception in her mother's womb to this very moment, and all the moments to follow, Onyx knew help was essential to the person she had grown to be, and she knew that God her Helper would continue to order her steps.

Let's Pause & Ponder, Let's Document & Discuss

1. Was Onyx justified in her assessment of the double standard in the workplace? Was the fact that she insisted on doing business without "playing the game" viewed as a weakness? Did she have to be somewhat "cutthroat" to succeed? Why or why not?

_____

_____

_____

_____

_____

2. Should Onyx have tried to convince Nyla not to listen to Darsi? Was that too much to expect from a fourth grader? Why or why not?

_____

_____

_____

_____

_____

3. Mr. Lincoln's job required him to travel constantly. How does a father make the decision between a lucrative position requiring him to be away from home versus accepting a lower salary but being home for dinner every night? What are the particulars that factor into that decision?

_____

_____

_____

_____

_____

4. Should Mrs. Rydington have used her influence to cover for Hudson? Why or why not? Does a parent's choice to intervene depend on the age of the child at the time of the offense?

_____

_____

_____

_____

_____

5. Did Onyx and Greg marry too soon? Would it have made any difference if they had dated longer? Why or why not? Is it possible to remain friends after a divorce? Is it even necessary? Why or why not?

_____

_____

_____

_____

6. Regarding the women's conference theme *To Speak or Not to Speak,* are you naturally more of a talker or more of a listener? Do you think your answer is based on your personality? On your upbringing? In our world of texting versus live conversation, which do you prefer? Why?

_____

_____

_____

_____

7. Onyx had a certain amount of power in her workplace. Influence can look a lot like power if it causes people to follow your agenda. Are you influential in any sphere of your life? In your family? With your friends? If so, do you sometimes find yourself using it to manipulate? Why or why not?

_____

_____

_____

_____

8. God is our Helper, and we want to reflect His qualities, so we want to be helpers. What is the difference between helping and enabling? If a family member is struggling financially and you are doing well, do you feel obligated to loan or give them money? Why or why not?

_____

_____

_____

_____

_____

MEET

Candace Sweete

*C*andace Sweete. Candee, the name she chose to go by, was the youngest of this friend group, though the four of them were separated only by months. Candee was quick-witted, she was outspoken, and she would often respond without first thinking about what she should say. And those responses could sometimes be abrasive. Her ready defense for such harsh delivery was that things needed to be said and that the truth needed to be told. And she had no problem being the one to tell it.

There are three 'e's in Candee's last name because she's a triple threat, 36-24-36, just the way The Commodores described in their hit song "Brick House". And her last name is pronounced "sweet", just like the stuff that kids love, good on their tongues, but bad for their teeth. With her temperament, she could have just as easily been named Candace *Storm*. With that ginger hair? And that fire in her eyes? Yes, Storm would have worked just as well.

Candee wanted desperately to love and to be loved. She sometimes displayed slivers of sensitivity and compassion, but they were often overshadowed by the bigger parts of her persona. Her skewed view of love. That she could be so easily angered. And Candee had deep-seated, preconceived notions about men, about physical intimacy, and about relationships of all kinds.

Candee accepted that sometimes she was treated as though her name sounded like a stage name. So much so that she thought it would have been normal for her to be a candy *stripper* rather than a hospital candy striper. With the exception of her physique, she had a very unhealthy view of who she was, and of her own self-worth.

Candee never allowed herself to look within, to possibly gain some insight into defining who she was. Could it be that she didn't believe there was anything to see? Although she was part of a family who were church-goers, she hadn't received what the bible says about her. Because of that, she never looked to God to define her. Her perspective was always based on the opinion of other people, and on their acceptance of who they thought she was.

Candee longed for her mother's guidance as it related to self-confidence. Regrettably, Ms. Clara was unable to provide it on any level, simply because she had never seen it. Self-assurance in any form had never been modeled for her.

When Candee was a child, Ms. Clara was excited about dressing her in cute little outfits, complete with lacey socks and matching bows in her hair. She loved lying on the floor, playing with her for what seemed like hours on end. But when it came to actually doing the hard work of being a parent, Ms. Clara preferred to leave the heavy lifting to Candee's father. Mr. Gerald was a good dad, but as good a dad as he was, he couldn't be her mother. In his mind, there were some lessons only mothers could teach their daughters.

CANDACE AND HER MOM, MS. CLARA

*C*andee was Ms. Clara's first-born daughter. Two more girls would follow, Shannon, when Candee was five, and Paula, when she was eight. For those first five years, Candee was the absolute center of attention, for both her parents. If they weren't working, or sharing a date night, they were spending time with her. But when her sisters were born, of course, that attention was divided by three.

As Candee grew from being a teenager into a young adult, it was evident that she had more of a creative nature. She was drawn to poetry and music and interpretive dance. Those inclinations dictated what career she wanted to pursue, unlike her sisters, who followed the "normal" paths of nursing and teaching. She could hear Ms. Clara's voice in her ear: "Now Candee, that dancing stuff is good for fun, but you need a *real* job". That comment only reinforced her belief that she was less than, which is why she briefly entertained the idea of working as an exotic dancer to earn extra money while in college. She felt less than, so she thought she might as well act less than.

After finishing college and working some years in the private sector, Candee followed her dream all the way to New York, where she opened a dance studio. She worked really hard to make CS Dance Moves a grade-A establishment, and her hard work paid off. She was given the opportunity to join a team consisting of seven women of color, chosen to organize and produce a Broadway play! Every aspect of the entire project would be managed by this team of sisters.

Three of the seven ladies in charge were several years Candee's senior. As God would have it, in addition to working relationships, Candee would come to develop friendships with these ladies. She felt comfortable letting her guard down because she felt no rivalry with them. These ladies had been there, done that, and had plenty to teach Candee. They shared that they had been show-stoppers in their day, and that as cute as she was, and as cute as they thought they were back then, there was, and always would be, someone just a little cuter. The point was not to trip. Just do you. For two reasons. One, you can't do anybody else. And two, nobody can do you like you can.

These were just a few of the invaluable nuggets of necessary knowledge Candee would glean from these ladies. She was glad she let them into her life. And she was glad to come to learn the unparalleled value of female friendship.

CANDACE AND HER DAD, MR. GERALD

Mr. Gerald doted on Candee, even after her sisters were born. He always told her how pretty she was, and he always made a big deal when she brought home straight A's on her report cards. Beyond being pretty and being smart, because Candee was the oldest, she was expected to set an example for her younger siblings. She was admittedly a bit selfish. She didn't appreciate being saddled with a responsibility she hadn't asked for. After all, she was perfectly happy being the only child. Nevertheless, she did her best to be the best big sister she could be.

Mr. Gerald was a good father, but he was pretty reserved. He wasn't a touchy-feely kind of dad, so Candee didn't know what positive male affection was, let alone what it was supposed to be. That, coupled with her father's more passive posture in the way he related to her mother, helped to shape how Candee looked back at men whenever men looked at her. She hadn't been taught that she needed to allow men to pursue her, not the other way around. She felt it was her job to get and to keep their attention, by any means necessary.

One of the privileges of being the oldest sibling in the Sweete household was the luxury of having your own space, while your two younger sisters shared a bedroom. As a teenager, Candee spent all of her free time in her bedroom, reading poetry books and listening to music.

Mr. Gerald noticed that Candee rarely, if ever, visited any of her classmates' homes or invited them to theirs. But he never asked why. He concluded that maybe his eldest daughter was just a loner. The apple hadn't fallen far from the tree since he, too, could be somewhat solitary. It was an attribute they shared. He didn't ask her many questions about her connection with other girls. His understanding of a father's relationship with his children, be they sons or daughters, was to be protector and provider, but not necessarily much else.

When Candee and her sisters were little girls, when Mr. Gerald could run and play with them, tickle and wrestle with them, he felt those interactions were appropriate. But as the girls got older, especially when they began physically transforming into young women, he stopped touching them altogether. He hadn't realized how important a kiss on the cheek or a warm embrace was. When offered from a place of pure love in the heart of a father for his daughters, not only was it fitting and proper, it was longed for and necessary, particularly at this stage of their lives.

When Candee would approach her dad for his thoughts on some issue she was facing, Mr. Gerald would steer her in the direction of her mother, believing Ms. Clara was more equipped to handle it. He felt his girls' development from adolescence and beyond was Ms. Clara's area of expertise, whatever the subject matter was. His contribution need only be to support what his wife thought was best.

CANDACE AND HER BESTIE, PHARR

*P*harr Campbell was Candee's best friend. Most girls' besties are girls, but Pharr was a guy. Of course, Candee interacted with girls, either while at work or at church, but she had no friendships with women. The voice in Candee's head told her they were jealous of her, which meant they could never be a real friend to her. After all, she had a cute, catchy nickname. She had a booming personality to go along with that booming body, and although those things may have been superficial, her confidence in them was real.

Ironically, Candee was jealous of Amber, another of this gang of four from Mrs. Langow's class at EEA. She often competed with Amber for attention, because of Amber's equally shapely body, not to mention her golden skin tone.

During their high school days, Candee felt the other girls had been more of a friend to Amber than they had been to her. And because of that, she rarely, if ever, shared her thoughts or feelings with any of them.

On the other hand, she was open and completely transparent with Pharr. He was a guy, so there was no competition. They often watched sitcoms together, and when they did, Candee would let out her loudest, heartiest belly laugh, sometimes before the audience laugh track chimed in. Even as the two of them laughed until their stomachs hurt, she could hear Ms. Clara chiding her, telling her a lady would never behave that way. A lady would never be so simple as to laugh out loud in the presence of a man. But there was no pretense between Candee and Pharr. So she dismissed those thoughts and laughed all the more.

Candee divulged her deepest, darkest secrets to Pharr. And when she was wounded or hurt, she would lay her head on his shoulder and just sob, sometimes uncontrollably.

Pharr was entirely focused on grad school, so dating was not currently a priority of his. He had no time for it. That being the case, there was never any drama with a girlfriend wondering why he was spending so much time with Candee. As an added bonus, psychology being Pharr's chosen field of study equipped him to help Candee work through a lot of her issues. She trusted him completely. She knew she could be *real* real with him because he would never betray that trust, no matter how horrid the things she shared with him.

Pharr was a great listener. He would only offer a response when Candee asked him for one, and then, only if he really believed it was welcomed.

CANDACE AND HER GUY, SLOANE

Sloane Sheppard. What a tall glass of water he was! Candee was unashamedly frank about her attraction to Sloane, and he, of course, took note of her looks. But something more fascinated him. He was interested in getting to know who she was from the inside out. He wanted to know who she was in her heart. In her mind. And she would soon learn there was so much more to him than merely what met her eyes.

Sloane stood 6 foot 5 and weighed 245 pounds. He was an entrepreneur and a restauranteur. His restaurant, Shepp's, was an up-and-coming hot spot in Denver. Shepp's was well known for good food and great jazz.

Candee was working as a media specialist, learning the ins and outs of social media in the marketplace. The job was demanding, but she liked it, and it paid the bills. But dance was her passion, and she remained laser focused on her dream of opening her own dance studio. Pharr was still in school, working on his master's in psychology. He and Candee both needed a break from their jam-packed schedules, so they agreed to treat themselves to a night on the town. They decided to go to Shepp's.

Sloane made his way around the restaurant, checking in with his patrons as he did every night. As he neared the area where Candee and Pharr were seated, he caught her in his peripheral vision. Just before he got to their table, Pharr's cellphone rang. He took the call, asked Candee to excuse him, and stepped into the adjacent hallway. Sloane asked Candee how dinner was and had she enjoyed the band. She replied, flirtingly, "very good" and "very much". They locked eyes for about five seconds, but it seemed more like five minutes. Just as Sloane was about to introduce himself, Pharr returned to the table, and still standing, told Candee he needed to leave but that he would call her before he turned in for the night. Before either Candee or Sloane could tell Pharr they hoped everything was all right, Pharr was halfway to the door. After formally introducing themselves, Candee and Sloane agreed to meet for lunch the next day.

Fast forward two years, after some deep soul-searching conversations with each other and with a Christian counselor, Sloane proposed to Candee. But he had one condition. He cautioned her not to give him an answer until she fully understood that she was sweet because of her heart. Not her looks. Not her body. Not her name. Her heart. And when he was convinced she understood that, they began planning their big day!

CANDACE AND HER CHURCH,
NEW HEARTS WORLD CHURCH

The Sweete Family had been a part of NHWC since Elder Mitchell B. Gillespie officiated over Ms. Clara and Mr. Gerald's wedding ceremony nearly 33 years ago. The five of them all served in some capacity at New Hearts. Candee and her mom were in the choir, Shannon and Paula were ushers, and Mr. Gerald worked with the new members' ministry. Candee enjoyed church, but truth be told, she could take it or leave it. She just couldn't believe people could actually be selfless servants, and certainly not to a God they couldn't see. But she knew nice girls went to church, so she rarely missed a Sunday.

Candee was also disillusioned by other church members who lived what she referred to as "double lives". She would overhear women slandering other women in the choir, saying things like "I *know* she didn't wear *that!*", not two seconds after hugging them and kissing them on the cheek. This only reinforced her anemic stance on female-to-female relationships. If women couldn't be trusted to be real in their interactions in the church, why would she trust any of them to be anything different anywhere else?

It was mid-August, and time again for Ministry Now, the church's annual ministry exhibition. Teams of two from each sector of the church would set up booths in the multi-purpose center, displaying life-size posters showing examples of how they served the church and the community. They also had hospitality bags that included a bottle of water, a handful of peppermints, a Starbucks gift card, and a pamphlet listing meeting dates and times, the ministry leader contact information, and a link with step-by-step instructions on how to connect to that ministry page on the church's website.

Madison Tolliver had been a member of NHWC for several months and had now decided to become a part of the choir. Candee was serving at the booth for the church choir, the Victorious Voices. The minute Madison walked up to the table, Candee sensed something genuine about her. She seemed unlike most of the other ladies Candee knew. After introducing herself as one of the choir's leaders, Candee handed Madison a bag, and told her to feel free to contact her if she had any questions or needed more information. And this time, Candee meant it. This time, that phrase wasn't just part of her script outline. And for the first time, she opened her mind to believe that not all women, especially not all the women at NHWC, led "double lives".

CANDACE AND HER INNER WOMAN

*C*andee avoided being honest with herself about herself. She would rather use her energies to uphold the façade she had created. It was just easier. It had worked so far. And it was less painful. It was Wednesday night, and having tipped in late after a long workday, Candee sat in the back. She allowed anything and everything to distract her from her pastor's probing words.

Elder Gillespie was preaching a sermon series on T.R.U.T.H., which was an acronym for "Telling it **R**ight to yo**U** and **T**o **H**im". The main point of the series was *always tell yourself the truth about yourself, so that when you hear it from someone else, it won't be a surprise, and you won't be offended.* That one was hard for Candee to swallow. She knew being honest would require a response, even if only in her mind and heart, and she was not willing to go there. She couldn't make herself disappear from the sanctuary, but she had gotten really good at shifting her mind away from uncomfortable realities. Even as the truth tried to invade her thinking, ushered in by Elder Gillespie's fiery presentation, she simply refused to think about what he was proclaiming.

Candee had a good heart. It was her mind that held her captive. She couldn't seem to shake those negative thoughts that kept popping up in her head. The thoughts that she didn't quite measure up; that she wasn't good enough. And she couldn't bring herself to believe in a life without constantly having to grapple with those thoughts. She just felt that facing the truth about the totality of her life as she believed it to be was more than she could take.

From Candee's vantage point, on the outside looking in, other women had seemingly perfect lives. They had perfect mothers and fathers. They had perfect boyfriends or husbands. Some even had perfect children. The fact that there were no perfect people and no such thing as perfection in any relationship didn't matter to Candee. That was her perception, and her perception was her reality. Hopefully, one day soon, she would be ready to allow her identity in Christ to penetrate her good heart and completely transform her mind. Unfortunately, she wasn't willing to let that day be today.

CANDACE AND GOD HER SAVIOR

*R*eal truth (which, by the way, is an oxymoron) has a way of slipping into your space. As great a life as Candee believed she had, there was still something needling her. Was she happy? Yes. Was she in love? Yes. But still, something wasn't quite right. She had to finally tell herself the truth. The *real* truth. She was incomplete. Something, or more accurately, Someone, was missing.

Things were so great with Sloane. He was a really good man, and the time they had spent together allowed her to see that. She had come to realize that there *were* a few good men. Not all men were players. Not all men were out for only themselves. Not all men wanted to use or abuse women. But this empty space, this cavity in her heart, was a void that even Sloane couldn't fill.

Candee had the safe haven of family with her parents and

sisters. She had the memory of childhood Sunday school lessons in Sis. Andrews' class. She had the scripture-filled Easter speeches that she could still recite verbatim. These all served as constant reminders of God's love, and giving her life to Him was the one and only thing that would make her whole. It was now clear to her: Total surrender to the Lord Jesus Christ was what was missing.

As a little girl, Candee had walked down the aisle to tell Elder Gillespie and the members of New Hearts that she wanted to be baptized. Being baptized, she thought as a child, was the way you became a member of the church. She wanted to sing in the choir, and she knew you had to be a member of the church to join the choir. But now she was an adult, and now she understood as an adult. Now, she wanted to be saved from her sins. Now she wanted to experience what she had heard so many others share about how they really *had* been "born again", that God's Holy Spirit really *will* empower you to "start over", just as she had read so many times before in II Corinthians 5:17:

Therefore, if anyone is in Christ, the new creation has come;
The old has gone, the new is here!

So she opened her ears to hear the Voice of God, and He spoke directly to her. She received Christ as Savior and Lord, and from that day to this one, her life would never be the same.

Let's Pause & Ponder, Let's Document & Discuss

1. Why do you think Candee had such a distorted view of what love is? Why do you think she was so angry and short-tempered? What does romantic love mean to you? Think of one thing that angers you. Why do you think it makes you angry?

_____

_____

_____

_____

_____

2. What do you think about the advice Candee's colleagues gave her? Do you think young women today are open to receiving advice from more senior women? Why or why not?

_____

_____

_____

_____

3. Do you think it's natural for fathers to relate more to sons and mothers to relate more to daughters? Why or why not? Should Candee's father have been more involved in her relationships with her peers? Why or why not?

_____

_____

_____

_____

_____

4. Candee and Pharr were best friends. Do you think males and females can have platonic relationships? Can they be best friends? Should they be? Why or why not? What would have to change when one or the other meets someone and enters into a romantic relationship?

_____

_____

_____

_____

_____

5. Candee was attracted to Sloane. Was it all right that she made the first move? Why or why not? What do you think of Sloane's proposal condition?

_____

_____

_____

_____

_____

6. Candee felt some of the women in her church were hypocrites. Have you ever felt that way? If so, what were the circumstances that prompted those feelings? Was the situation addressed and/or resolved?

_____

_____

_____

_____

_____

7. It was easier for Candee to believe the negative thoughts about who she was than to believe what God said about her. What steps can we take to believe God and reject negative thoughts? How can we help a friend or family member who may be struggling in this area?

_____

_____

_____

_____

_____

8. Candee finally realized what, or rather Who, was missing from her life. What are some of the trappings of "the good life" that may keep one from desiring a genuine relationship with God?

_____

_____

_____

_____

_____

MEET

Lorraine Lotaven Crowe

*L*orraine Lotaven Crowe. Lorraine had been named for her Aunt Lorraine, her "Aunt Rainey", who was her mom's identical twin sister. But everyone called her Ven, short for Lotaven, her paternal grandfather. Ven had a wide, bright smile that could light up any room. And she had eyes that were big and beautiful and brown and kind.

Ven loved her auntie, but she felt Lorraine was just too much name. She would never say it out loud, and she meant no disrespect, but she thought Lorraine sounded old. Upon graduating from college, she thought her name, when seen on her resume, might be some kind of red flag to certain hiring managers. She thought Ven, when written, and when spoken, appeared to be hip and unique.

Ven tended to be a little extra in her approach to most things; a little melodramatic. The truth was, her outlook on the whole name thing was probably non-existent to most people, or at the very least, not at all a big deal. But she thought it was, so she thought it best to err on the side of caution. Better safe than sorry, she reasoned.

Ven was a Type A personality, a perfectionist for sure, and was honest about her leanings toward attention deficit disorder. She hadn't been diagnosed, and she didn't view A.D.D. in a negative way. But she *did* acknowledge that she would begin working on a project, go into another room to get something she needed, and when she walked into the room, a photo of her and an old friend would catch her eye.

Just before reaching for the item she went in for, she'd wonder how life was treating her photo friend, and what she might be doing right now. She would stop, grab her phone, shoot a quick "just thinking about you" text message, then pick up the item she needed and head back to complete her task.

Being artistic in nature, Ven never denied any of her idiosyncrasies. To the contrary. She chose to embrace them. All of them. She knew they were just different parts of the whole of who she was. These traits may be labeled as oddities by some, but her self-confidence allowed her to see them as ways to enrich her contributions to the world she was living in.

Ven's plan for her foreseeable future was to work in real estate, as well as open an interior design firm. She thought it prudent to first work with an established company and gain some real-time, on-the-job experience. The time-tested tips and tricks she could obtain would only prove to make her that much more successful in her own company.

Ven's dad often told her he thought her initials, L.L.C., meant she would own a limited liability corporation, and a thriving one at that. He wasn't sure how it would come to be, but he believed her initials were an omen. They meant she was born to be the boss.

LORRAINE AND HER MOM, MS. LORETTA

When Dr. Harris informed the Crowes they would be welcoming a daughter, they decided her first name would be Lorraine, but Mr. Carl asked Ms. Loretta to let him choose Lorraine's middle name. She agreed, and on April 20th, at 6:48 a.m., Lorraine Lotaven Crowe was born. The name Lotaven was special to Mr. Carl because it was his father's name.

To her father, Ven was short for Lotaven. But to Ms. Loretta, Ven was really short for lavender, because Ven had always been such a sweet, quiet baby. As a mom, Ms. Loretta thought it was her job to calm her baby girl, but that was never necessary. In fact, the opposite proved to be true. Holding Ven, talking to her and singing to her, seemed to relax Ms. Loretta, lessening stresses in both her mind and her body. Spending time with her baby was sometimes synonymous with the "me time" she knew she needed to regularly take for herself.

From the day Ven was born, she and Ms. Loretta had a very special bond, and their bond only grew deeper as Ven grew older. Ms. Loretta knew of many mothers and daughters who oftentimes shared tense exchanges. Especially during those tricky teenage years, when every 16-year-old girl thinks she knows more about life than her mother could ever learn. For some, that strenuous period was just part of a daughter growing up. For others, it was the balance of her maturing and coming into her own. And her mother realizing she needed to let go so her daughter could do just that. Fortunately, Ven and her mom were able to strike that balance, and they remained very close, even as their relationship continued to grow and change, as it was bound by life to do.

Ms. Loretta and Ven both looked forward to the course Ven had charted for her life. They were excited about what life would be like when Ven became a career woman, when she became a wife, and when she became a mother. And they eagerly anticipated the many ways those life experiences would enhance their relationship. Ms. Loretta had to admit, she had an ulterior motive for when Ven began her season of motherhood. She could hardly *wait* to meet and spoil those grandbabies!

Ven was a source of pride and joy for both her parents,

and she had indeed become the young lady they raised her to be. They beamed with pride and gratitude every time they thought about the woman she was, and they continued to be as much a part of her life as they had always been.

LORRAINE AND HER DAD, MR. CARL

*s a naval officer, Ven's dad, Lieutenant Carl Crowe, was always punctual, and always precise. As a father, he appreciated that Ven wanted to turn her passion into her livelihood. Still, it was difficult for him to understand the delays that were sometimes inevitable with the real estate business, especially the construction side. Whether it was an equipment malfunction, a problem with a supply order, or having to wait out a pop-up thunderstorm, things happened. He felt those slowdowns might cause major setbacks, setbacks that would adversely affect Ven's bottom line, which would no doubt eat into her income.

Mr. Carl was a lifelong military man, and in the Navy, you always expected, and prepared for, the unexpected. Military life was like a well-oiled machine, and everything adhered to strict schedules and guidelines. There were no excuses, no negotiations, and no such thing as a Plan B. In other words, all the things Ven's career choice was not.

Ven's college major was business management, with an emphasis on real estate. She had a clear career objective: to work in real estate and interior design, working for herself. Her formal training, coupled with her innate gift of a good eye for home décor, was a recipe for success.

Mr. Carl would rather Ven had chosen to build a Fortune 500 company, earning a six- to seven-figure salary. He always knew she'd be the boss, but he had envisioned her as the CEO of a huge corporation on Wall Street. Not owning an interior design firm and selling real estate. But he loved his daughter, and he saw how happy it made her.

Ven not only gave her clients houses, she gave them beautiful houses. She had a hand in helping to make those houses homes, and in making them comfortable places for creating great memories.

Mr. Carl truly only wanted what was best for Ven. He came to accept that his dream was not hers, and the choices he might make wouldn't always be the same ones she made. It *was* her life, after all. When he came to terms with that, he knew Ven was exactly where she was supposed to be. And he couldn't have been more proud.

LORRAINE AND HER BESTIE, RAEGAN

*V*en met Raegan Robinson in kindergarten on the playground of Cooper Elementary. Raegan's mom and Ven's dad were both Naval officers, and both their families had been stationed in San Diego, California. The girls would meet at the swings every day for two weeks before they learned they lived on the same street, just one block from one another!

Ven and Raegan were inseparable. They did everything together. Sleepovers, tea parties, playing dress up, and learning to ride their bicycles. You would rarely ever see one and not see the other.

The Robinsons had some exciting news to share, so they invited the Crowe family over for dinner. Commander Robinson had been promoted to captain, but it came with a reassignment to a different state. Both girls' parents and older siblings had gotten used to military life; they were used to moving. It was par for the course. But Ven and Raegan were so young. They had lived their entire five-year-old lives a few houses apart on Waterside Drive. They just couldn't understand why they would no longer see each other every day.

Ven cried for three days straight. She missed her friend terribly. Even though they lived in a world of texts and tweets, their grandmothers had taught them the lost art of letter writing. So they wrote each other often. They video chatted, too, but it just wasn't the same.

As the girls matured and their lives became more and more occupied, they continued to communicate, just not as much as they would have liked. Ven's family was still living in Cali, but Raegan's family was now living in Texas. Ven and Raegan each applied to various colleges, hoping they would maybe end up in the same state, or at least geographically close enough to meet for an occasional girls' weekend. The challenge would be to synchronize their schedules.

As fate would have it, they were both accepted to Florida A&M University. The girls took education very seriously. They had been taught that it was the basis for whatever career path they chose. Attending a historically black university was just icing on the cake.

Ven and Raegan were so excited to learn they would be classmates again. They were the best of friends as kindergarteners at Cooper Elementary, and thirteen years later, they would have the chance to become best friends all over again.

LORRAINE AND HER GUY, KEITH

*fter college, Ven accepted a position working for Your Indoor Treatment located in Charlotte, North Carolina. Having moved up through the ranks of the company, she was ready to open her own interior design firm. She even had a name for it: Incomparable Interior Designs. Ven felt really good about all she had learned at YIT, and she knew she was ready. But Ven was a smart, forward-thinking girl, and she thought, in addition to beautifying homes for her clients, why not find the properties as well? So it was decided. Before submitting her resignation, she would secure her real estate license. The additional six months to a year would give her the opportunity to put everything in place for the launch of her business. Ven understood becoming the boss would mean twice as much work and half as much time to do all of everything. Being proactive and getting as many of her ducks in a row as possible beforehand would make for a smoother start.

Ten months had passed, and Ven received her final assignment with YIT. She was tasked with managing a staging project for a home in a newly constructed subdivision. After making note of the address and grabbing her tablet, she headed to the property. When she arrived, there were landscapers working outside and subcontractors working inside. She noticed a van parked on the street with "KMac Construction Company" painted on its side in bright orange letters.

The front door of the property was open, so she walked in, took out her tablet, and started jotting down ideas as to what artwork would look good in what room, which area rugs should go where, and how many indoor plants would be needed to add just enough splashes of green. As she turned to leave the family room and head into the kitchen, the huge wall over the fireplace caught her eye, and she quickly spun back around. Looking at the wall a second time, she remembered a piece of three-dimensional art in the company inventory. *Yes*, she thought. *That's the perfect spot for that piece.*

Just as she was passing the dining area, a gentleman was walking backwards while directing two workers to where a large beam was to be placed. He bumped right into her! He apologized profusely, but Ven really didn't mind. He was kinda cute. He told her he didn't know anyone other than crew members would be there. She told him she was with

Your Indoor Treatment, and explained that she was making preparations for staging. He told her he had worked with YIT before, apologized again, and continued with instructing the workers. Ven was now in the kitchen, deciding what items would be used there. But she was watching this guy, and she was hanging on his every word. He was not a team lead or a supervisor. He was, without question, the man in charge.

By the time Ven returned to the office, Keith, the guy whom she had collided with, had already called Mark Tillerman, one of the co-owners of YIT. It had been some time since Keith and Mark had worked together, so after exchanging pleasantries, Keith asked who was managing the staging at 717 Parkington Place. When Mark told him her name was Ven Crowe, and that she had been with the company for the past six years, Keith's response was, "Why haven't I met her?" Mark chuckled, and then agreed to pass Keith's number on to Ven. She would later learn he was Keith McNeal, the owner of KMac Construction Company, and the owner of the van with the bright orange letters. Keith had begun his business nearly five years ago, flipping houses. Now he was one of the most sought-after homebuilders in Charlotte.

Just as Ven was getting home, Keith called. They spent the next two hours on the phone, laughing, talking, and getting to know each other. Interestingly enough, they found they had quite a bit in common.

The past year had been a busy one for Ven. She had

obtained her real estate license, found office space for her business, and designed and furnished it impeccably. She hired one full-time worker and two part-time college students as her first employees, and she had already procured contracts with three clients. Incomparable Interior Designs was born. Ven's dream had become a reality.

Just before opening day, Ven was offered deep discounts on some principal furniture pieces from a company that was relocating. Phabulous Phurnishings was liquidating larger items to make for an easier transition. The pieces were extremely opulent and would be for Ven's more elite clientele. She knew having these pieces would increase her income percentage, but she had been asked to accept the items off the books. It was unethical, but it would work to her advantage in the form of a tax break. After all, she had overhead, and she had utilities. She had employees, and she had insurance. And as a sole proprietor, she was responsible for all of it. She thought: *A woman's gotta do what a woman's gotta do, right?* But then she thought, almost immediately: *If I start out wrong, how can I expect to end up right?* She took a hard pass.

Keith and Ven spent as much time together as possible, but it was challenging. Having lived the experience of starting a business from only a vision in his head and a dream in his heart, Keith was very much aware of what was required. He was aware of how taxing the whole process would be on Ven. He knew the long hours would exhaust her, both mentally and physically. But he was very clear: He wanted to be with her. And even though sometimes Ven was so tired she couldn't see straight, she felt the same way.

Somehow, they made it work. That they were able to build a relationship at the same time Ven was building her business was a testament to the kind of man Keith was. He wasn't pushy and he wasn't needy. He knew they would get there. And he was right.

Over the next eighteen months, as Incomparable Interior Designs became the firm nearly every homebuyer called, Keith and Ven not only became man and wife, they also merged their businesses. Keith found the land and built the homes. Ven sold the homes and dressed them stunningly. Incomparably.

LORRAINE AND HER CHURCH, THIRD AVENUE AME CHURCH

*V*en was just an infant when her family was relocated to San Diego. Though she had nothing to compare it to, she found comfort in having grown up as a member of a church that understood how fluid military life could be. Third Avenue AME was a small, close-knit congregation. Every family in the church had at least one person who was either active duty or an enlisted reserve. They had all learned to hold on lovingly but loosely to their relationships. That a family might be transferred to a different state, or if it was a special assignment, maybe even a different country, was always a real possibility. Ironically, it taught them to hold fast to what mattered most, namely sharing, caring, and not taking anything or anyone for granted.

Pastor Douglass encouraged the church to be there for

one another. He implored them to be helping hands and listening ears to aid each other in navigating life's twists and turns. He reminded them to always share a smile or a hug. To take the time to say kind words to each other. And he would tell them that even if your words were few, to make those few words count. He would often say, "When it comes to words, it's not quantity, it's quality". Ven viewed that advice as her pastor's interpretation of 'less is more' , especially when it comes to what we *say* versus what we *do*.

While they were dating, Keith attended Third Avenue with Ven. But when they became engaged, they decided to search for a new place of worship together. So they began visiting other churches. The non-negotiables were that the congregation believed in Jesus Christ as Lord, without question, and that the Word of God be taught with clarity and conviction.

After about nine and a half weeks, they agreed Pathway Fellowship was the place for them. From the first time they worshipped there, one thing was apparent: the spiritual foundation that had been lain for Ven as a child and reinforced as a young adult at Third Avenue was mirrored at Pathway. Growing individually and as a couple was important to both Ven and Keith. They believed they had found a church that would offer the practical tools needed to develop their walk with Christ, and that they would have true support and accountability in their desire to become more mature Christians. And they looked forward to learning how to do marriage the right way. God's Way.

LORRAINE AND HER INNER WOMAN

*henever she took an introspective view of herself, she was Lorraine. When she was more chilled, she was Ven. Even when she was more light-hearted and less serious, in her mind and in her heart, Ven always believed one thing: being a person of character was the only kind of person to be. She had been taught the differ-ence in reputation and character. The former is who the proverbial "they" say you are. The latter is who you *really* are. Ven relished reminiscing and musing about good times from "back in the day". It made her happy to think about the good ol' days. She had a mind like an elephant, and when she would daydream, she could recall each and every detail. She could tell you who was there and who was not, who said what and who said nothing at all. Whenever friends or family struggled to recall names or dates or places, they knew exactly who could fill in the blanks.

Sometimes Ven wished life could be the way it was when ignorance really *was* bliss. Before she learned of its ups and downs. She'd say to herself, "Wouldn't it be nice to go back? To go back to a time when life was simple and good?" She knew it was okay to look back, maybe for a quick glance, but she knew she couldn't *go* back. She knew if things stayed the same, she would never be challenged. She would never grow. She would never grow physically. She would never grow mentally. She would never grow emotionally. And she most certainly would never grow spiritually. She knew you couldn't move forward while at the same time, looking back. And she was a better woman because of that realization.

Still, sometimes she recalled how, as her younger self, she had begrudged the times her family was relocated throughout her dad's career. She remembered how Pastor Douglass seemed to relentlessly admonish them to hold on to people and places and relationships with a delicate grip. Now that she was a grown-up, she understood why. It was because stringent rules, along with necessary realignments, were central to the world of military life.

But her life was different now. Now that she and Keith were married, Ven could fully appreciate that the two of them had become one. She no longer needed to concern herself with whatever antipathy she may have felt as the child of a military parent. She was Keith's life partner, and as such, she had a voice in how they responded to the changes life would bring their way. And, with all due respect to Pastor Douglass, she *could* hold on to Keith, tightly, and she would never have to let him go. At least not any time soon.

LORRAINE AND GOD HER PEACE

*F*or as long as Ven could remember, the second week of July had always been designated as the week for vacation bible school at Third Avenue. During her childhood and throughout her teenage years, she hadn't missed one session. Ven loved VBS, and she looked forward to attending every summer. One year, in particular, would completely alter the way she viewed her relationship with God.

This summer, Sis. Duncan was assigned to teach the Upper Teen Girls' class. The class was named "upper teen" because these girls were 16-, 17- and 18-year-olds. They were no longer girls. They had grown into young ladies. Since these ladies were a bit more mature, Sis. Duncan considered herself more a facilitator than a teacher.

The chosen topic for study and discussion was *The 9*

Names of Jehovah God. VBS was held Sunday through Thursday evenings at 6:30. Sis. Duncan decided they would cover two names per night for the first four nights. On Thursday night, the final night, they would cover the ninth name. After using the first half of the class time to discuss the ninth Name of God, they would conclude their time together with each girl sharing which Name of God meant the most to her.

Sis. Duncan handed each girl a list of the nine names and their meanings. After reading through the handout, Ven felt drawn to Jehovah Shalom, the Lord is Peace. She looked forward to learning about all nine, but she believed Jehovah Shalom would mean the most to her. There seemed to be a connection between her calm temperament and the peace that only God provides. She always knew there was a reason she responded thoughtfully rather than reacted irrationally to whatever life brought her way. She knew there was a reason she literally trusted God with everything and everyone. And since she believed there were no coincidences in life, she trusted the connection she felt. The peace that passes all understanding was just one of the many gifts she now possessed because of her decision to invite Christ to live inside her heart, and to be Lord over her life.

So when it was her turn, Ven shared her choice with the class. With great enthusiasm, she declared, "Jehovah Shalom. The Lord is Peace. The Lord is my peace!"

Let's Pause & Ponder, Let's Document & Discuss

1. Did Lorraine (Ven) have a legitimate concern with the whole "name" thing? Would potential employers assume *Lorraine* might be an older applicant? Or was she really just being extra? Why or why not?

_____

_____

_____

_____

2. Ven and Ms. Loretta were able to coexist as mother and daughter *and* as friends. What are practical ways mothers and adult daughters can cultivate healthy relationships? How should parents react when their adult son or daughter makes a choice contrary to the Word of God? Contrary to the ethics and morals they were taught while growing up?

_____

_____

_____

_____

3. Ven's dad believed she had an exceptional mind and thought she chose a career beneath her capability. Why do parents sometime pressure their children to fulfill the parents' dreams? How do children oppose those expectations while still honoring their mother and father?

_____

_____

_____

_____

_____

4. In a world of reality TV stars and YouTube celebrities, how do parents instill in children the importance of a college education? If a child prefers a career as a comedian rather than a doctor, should you necessarily steer him or her toward the latter? As you support their dream, should you convince them to get a degree as a Plan B? Why or why not?

_____

_____

_____

_____

_____

5. When it came to his relationship with Ven, Keith wasn't pushy or needy. He trusted that, in time, what they shared would grow. Does a guy need to be relentless in his pursuit to prove he's interested? What does that look like? What do you think about a guy frequently calling or texting you? Does it flatter you that he wants you to spend all of your free time with him? Why or why not?

_____

_____

_____

_____

6. If each has strong ties to their respective churches, should a couple find a new place of worship, or should the wife be expected to join her husband at his church? Why or why not?

_____

_____

_____

_____

_____

7. Ven had a clear understanding of the difference between reputation and character. Does it concern you what others think of you? If so, to what degree? Is it important to you that people like you? Why or why not?

_____

_____

_____

_____

8. Jehovah Shalom, the Lord is Peace, was the Name of God that meant the most to Ven. The other eight names of God the class explored were *The Lord My Banner, The Lord My Shepherd, The Lord Who Heals, The Lord is There, The Lord Our Righteousness, The Lord Who Sanctifies You, The Lord Will Provide,* and *The Lord of Hosts.* Which name means the most to you? Why?

_____

_____

_____

_____

MEET

Amber
Autumn Grace

*A*mber Autumn Grace. A golden-skinned, good-looking girl with "body for days" as John Legend would say. She was a curvy girl who wore her clothes well, and they wore her. Her thick hourglass figure showed through, but she didn't put her body on display. Amber had it, but she never flaunted it. She was always a lady. She had inherited her curves from her mother, and her mother from her mother. It was in her genes, *and* in her jeans. Her GeeGee would often tell her, "Li'l girl, you would look good in a potato sack".

As is true with many pretty people, Amber was prejudged. She was prejudged because of what people saw when they looked at her. She was prejudged, by both men and women. By what they thought, and by what they themselves perceived when they looked at her. Not because of anything she had said or done, but because of their own misconceptions.

Women prejudged Amber from a place of petty jealousy, because they didn't have her body, or her skin, or her hair. Men prejudged her with the assumption that she was "that kind of girl", simply based on what she looked like on the outside. The sad truth was that it was a loss for both men and women, because neither would make the effort to get to know her.

Amber was a wonderful person. She was friendly, and she was pleasant to be around. She believed her affable disposition was a gift from God, and for that she was sincerely grateful. Being cordial. Being approachable. Just being nice. She thought these elements were Christ-like. She knew they were favorable attributes that would add to her being a suitable helpmate for her future husband. And anyone who knew her would tell you, there is no word to describe the kind of friend Amber was to those in her small sister circle.

Amber was the kind of friend who would always be there. When she said, "If you need me, call me", she wasn't just saying what a friend was supposed to say. She meant it. If you needed her, she would be on your doorstep. Amber would be there whether you needed a sounding board, a shoulder to cry on, or someone to share a gallon of Blue Bell.

Friendships were important to Amber, so if there were disagreements or skirmishes between girlfriends, she would be the peacemaker. She would be the one to insist that they come together, face to face, confront the issue head on, and resolve it. Expeditiously.

Following law school, Amber went to work as a criminal defense attorney. She had such zeal for the law. She was fascinated by how laws were drafted. Beyond exercising her right to vote, which she strongly believed in, Amber felt, to make a real difference, to be a part of how laws are actually legislated, she would need to be elected to Congress.

After thinking more about it, she concluded that casting her ballot in support of those representatives whose agendas aligned more closely with her own, might be the better way to see fair laws legislated. For Amber, becoming an attorney would be her way of making sure justice was actually implemented.

Amber saw up close and personal how out of balance the scales of justice were when it came to what was meted out to people of color. The vilification was often overt, and she felt she had to be their voice. If she didn't speak for them, she feared they would never be heard. Amber always had a heart for the down-trodden and the disenfranchised. Sitting on that side of the courtroom, acting as their advocate, was a perfect fit. It was as natural for her as breathing.

AMBER AND HER MOM, MS. ANNA

$\mathcal{M}$s. Anna, Amber's mother, and Ms. Alice, her grandmother, or as Amber called her, "Gee-Gee", were both just as attractive as Amber was. Ms. Anna was in her mid-50s and had always been a gorgeous woman. She had been a model in her 20s and 30s, and even now, continued to be pursued by top agencies. And Ms. Alice, now elderly, still epitomized all that is majestic and regal.

During one of their mother-daughter talks, Ms. Anna shared some things from her past with Amber that she hadn't shared before. She told Amber that for many years of her own life, she had been the subject of gossip and whispers, simply because of her appearance. She told Amber that she would often overhear phrases like "I guess the thinks she's something special" and "she thinks she's all that". "First of all," Ms. Anna said, "how is it that someone actually believed they knew what was in another person's thoughts?" "And secondly", she continued, "the fact that someone would make such a remark is clear evidence of what *that* person was thinking". Ms. Anna believed that not only are such quips telling of what is in that person's *mind*, it also validates what's in their heart. Whenever Ms. Anna was met with such verbal insults, they brought Matthew 12:34b to mind:

For the mouth speaks what the heart is full of.

Ms. Anna knew exactly how to cope with those paltry attempts at bullying. She knew that hurt people hurt people, and most of the time, they really didn't even know why. She told Amber all bullies know is that they feel uncertain about themselves and consequently, about everybody else. They are the personification of misery loving company.

To combat those slights and slurs, Ms. Anna simply reminded herself of what God said about her. And she admonished Amber to do the same. She taught her daughter to be beautiful on the inside. She cautioned her to remember that it didn't matter if an apple was red and shiny on the outside if it was rotten on the inside. Ms. Anna raised Amber to be confident, but not conceited. She raised her to be assured, but not arrogant. Whenever she spoke with her daughter about healthy self-esteem, she balanced her advice with Luke 14:11:

For all those who exalt themselves will be humbled,
and those who humble themselves will be exalted.

"And Amber, above all else", she would tell her, "be true to who you are, and to who God created you to be". Those words gave Amber the aplomb she needed to stand strong on her principles, even if it meant she stood out.

AMBER AND HER DAD, MR. JAKE

*One of the reasons Ms. Anna insisted her daughter be a strong woman was because Amber's father was absent for just about all of her upbringing. Jake and Anna were teenage parents who never married, but they both loved Amber deeply. Because they were so young when Amber was born, it was almost as though they had a baby sister to play with. The responsibility, not to mention the bandwidth of caring for another human being, never even entered their not-yet-mature minds.

When Mr. Jake was thirteen, his older brother Christopher was a victim of gun violence, killed in a drive-by shooting between rival gangs. Jake and Christopher were three years apart and were very, very close. Jake looked up to his older brother, and he wanted to do everything Chris did, exactly the way Chris did it. He would get so frustrated when he couldn't just as easily conquer whatever new skill Chris had just mastered.

Mr. Jake was never quite the same after Christopher died. He started to make reckless decisions. He began skipping school. He began experimenting with drugs. He began spending time with the very kinds of youngsters who had taken his brother's life.

One ill-fated Saturday night, Jake made the horrible choice to join his new friends Melvin and Tony in their plan to rob F&P's, a neighborhood convenience store. Melvin and Tony were both older than Jake. And since Jake was so easily influenced, they persuaded him to be the lookout guy. Their rationale was in the event Jake choked and got caught, the two of them could get away. They didn't feel bad about abandoning him. They figured the system would go easier on Jake because of his age.

Melvin and Tony convinced themselves that if they weren't able to pull this off, Jake wouldn't be tried as an adult. He wouldn't have to spend any time in prison. He would just be sent to a juvenile detention center. It wouldn't really affect him. They imagined that after a few years, it would be as if it never happened, and that Jake would simply go on with the rest of his life.

Jake stood near the front door of the store as Melvin approached the counter. If Jake saw any police officers in the area or approaching the store, he was to open the door, causing the doorbell to chime. That sound was the signal for Melvin to abort the plan. Melvin brandished his weapon for the clerk to see. No words needed to be spoken. The clerk knew exactly why Melvin showed him the gun, and he knew what was expected of him once he saw it.

At the very moment the register opened, flashing lights and blaring sirens could be seen and heard. The police had been dispatched to Earl's Gas Station next door. Assuming the clerk had pressed the silent alarm button, Melvin panicked and shot the clerk in the chest, at point blank range.

Tony was behind the wheel of the getaway car, with the motor running. Something inside his head told him to drive. Fast. So he sped off at the sight of the first police cruiser. After having been told the alarm at Earl's had been tripped accidentally, and no police presence was needed, Tony's screeching tires alerted the officers to F&P's. So they sprinted over. They met Melvin as he was running toward the door. They wrestled him to the floor and cuffed him. As for Jake, it was as if his shoes were nailed to the ground. He just froze. He couldn't even find the strength to speak, let alone run. He was also placed in handcuffs, walked across the parking lot, and placed in the back of a squad car, without incident.

This all happened just before Amber's fourth birthday. Mr. Jake was sentenced to thirty years in prison. His court-appointed attorney believed the sentence was excessive, but the fact that the clerk was killed didn't leave much room to negotiate any possible plea.

As she got older, Amber started to ask questions about

her dad. She had faint memories of his visits, and she wondered why those visits had stopped so abruptly. Ms. Anna thought Amber was now old enough to handle her father's story. So she sat Amber down and told her the whole of everything, including what happened to her Uncle Chris, and the effect it had on her dad's life.

After hearing all her mom had to say, in an instant, Amber made the decision to become a criminal defense attorney. She would argue vigorously for impartial rulings, and she would work hard to ensure the punishment always fit the crime. And above all else, she would make it her mission to have her father released, even if it shaved only a few years off his sentence.

AMBER AND HER BESTIE, BAILEIGH

*A*mber and Baileigh were eighth graders at EEA. They made friends almost instantly because they had so much in common. They were both dedicated to physical fitness, which meant adhering to a regular exercise regimen and eating right. To these girls, taking care of one's body should be regarded as a lifelong practice. They believed spiritual health was paramount, and physical health allowed you to be able and available to do your best for God.

Amber and Baileigh signed up for the school's track team, but they also shared an affinity for mental aptitude. They could hardly wait to become freshmen, because then they would be eligible to join the debate team. That eighth-grade school year came and went lightning fast. They had prepared themselves by participating in online mock debates. And they were both ready to try out.

Amber was a natural debater, which is probably why she was so intrigued with trial law. She would often picture herself arguing cases for her defendants, painting colorful pictures for the judge and jury to see. And Baileigh, though she was studying to become a scientist, had the mind of a statistician. It was mesmerizing to watch her slice and dice facts and figures, presenting each of them with clean and clear precision. Once the girls were placed on a team, it was nearly impossible to find opponents who could successfully debate them, let alone defeat them.

One of the reasons Amber and Baileigh got along so well and became such close friends was that they each knew exactly who she was. And who the other was. They saw no *need* to be validated by others. They appreciated validation, and they graciously accepted it. But they never sought it. It wasn't something either of them had to have.

Amber was used to having her friendship mistrusted or even distrusted. She was often accused of being a fake. She was accused of being phony. She was accused of being too goody-goody, just because she was a nice person. And she *was* a nice person. But she was also straightforward.

Amber didn't play games, and she didn't entertain foolishness, or fools, for that matter. Whenever anyone offered to engage Amber in gossip, she would shut it down with the quickness. She refused to add to any rumor mill. In fact, she would boldly speak out against such blather. It finally occurred to her: the criticism of those who questioned the authenticity of her ability to be a friend was just a manifestation of their own insecurities. Simply put, they probably never knew what it was like to have a true friend, let alone be one.

In Amber's mind, a true friend doesn't gossip about you. A real friend will no doubt disagree with you from time to time, and she may challenge you a lot of the time. She might even take you to task if she feels you are stepping out of bounds. Amber wanted to be that kind of friend. She wanted to be the kind of friend described in Proverbs 27:6a:

Faithful are the wounds of a friend
[who corrects out of love and concern].

Amber's bestie Baileigh cared very little, if she cared at all, about what other people thought of her. She cared even less what other *girls* thought of her. In her experience, girls were just messy and not worth the trouble. But she was so grateful to have a true friend in Amber. Baileigh always said she'd rather have one Amber than ten dubious anybody-elses.

AMBER AND HER GUY, PATRICK

*B*aileigh was headed to DC to visit her parents, but stopped to have lunch with Amber on her way to the airport. They met at Lucy's, a quaint little outdoor café on Sixth Street. Just as they hugged and said their good-byes, Amber caught a glimpse of a guy catching a glimpse of her. He was dining alone, and he and his server were laughing and talking about last night's football game. Amber was a huge football fan, but she was still a girly girl. She embraced her hips, she kept gloss on her lips, and polish on her fingertips. And the football guy noticed.

Patrick Zeller, a well-known prosecutor, had just joined Henson, Carrington & Rhodes. Amber worked for Watson & Vickers. W&V and HCR sometimes worked together on special litigations. Amber thought she had seen Patrick around the building, but there *were* 35 floors. And since she was so consumed with the case she was currently working on, she hardly had time to look up. Until she had to.

The elevator reached her floor, and the doors opened. As she was walking off, Patrick was walking on. Their eyes locked, and they both had that same look on their faces. That look that said, without a word, "Didn't I see you at Lucy's the other day?"

Patrick stepped off the elevator and decided to wait for another one. After introductions and a little shop talk, he just put himself out there. "May I call you?", he said. Amber was kinda quiet, but she wasn't shy. "May I have your phone?", she replied. Her response caught him a little off guard, but he would never let her know that. He reached inside his jacket pocket, pulled out his phone, and handed it to her. Amber keyed in her name and number, handed his phone back to him, and walked away. As the next elevator arrived and the doors opened, Patrick said in a slightly raised voice, "I'll call you tonight". Hearing no response, he stepped onto the elevator. Just before the doors closed, he heard Amber say, "I'll answer on the third ring". He just smiled.

The following day, Amber had a full schedule. Patrick had convinced her she shouldn't start her day without a good breakfast. "After all", he would advise her, "it *is* the most important meal of the day". His day would be just as busy, so they agreed to go into their respective offices, organize their documents for the day's cases, and then meet at the small eatery on the first floor of their building. They enjoyed more great conversation, got to know each other even better, and made plans to attend the Seahawks game on Sunday.

Patrick not only had a reputation of being a playboy, he *was* a playboy. And he never tried to hide it. But when he met Amber, things changed for him. The more time they spent together, the more time he wanted them to spend together. He couldn't put it into words, but he knew there was something different about Amber. She was special. Very special. For the first time, he was not being pursued by the "flavor of the month", which was his description of whichever young lady he was dating at the moment. The tables had turned. Now *he* was the one texting throughout the day. Sometimes, there was even a heart emoji attached.

Amber hadn't dated a lot. Sure, there were guys she had gone out with. But none of those dates had led to anything remotely serious. She had set life goals, and she was focused on reaching them. Go to college, check. Go to law school, check. Pass the bar, check. Become an attorney, check. She was determined to be able to take care of herself, and take care of herself well. Amber's vision for her life always included marriage and family, but she was determined to get that law degree first.

Amber was falling in love with Patrick, and he was falling in love with her. But they hadn't talked about a future together. He wasn't quizzing her family or friends, trying to find out if she was thinking about marriage. Nor was she fantasizing about an intimate restaurant dinner where Patrick orders champagne, and her flute just happens to have a diamond ring sitting at the bottom of it. However, the closer they became, the more he felt that now might be a good time to at least ask Baileigh if Amber had mentioned marriage. And also to get her ring size.

Patrick was quite the chef. He remembers acting as his Granddaddy Matt's sous chef while listening to stories of his grandfather's cooking. Not only was Matt the neighborhood barbecue king, but before retiring, he spent 20 years managing the culinary team as the executive chef of The Golden Palate restaurant. Matt had learned to cook all kinds of foods, from Chicken Cordon Bleu to a perfectly flavored filet mignon. Patrick believed those skills were in his head and in his hands. And even in his blood.

On a Friday evening with flawless weather and a full moon, Patrick had prepared an amazing dinner for Amber. The wine was chilled, the candles were lit, and the fragrance of fresh flowers filled the air. They would be dining on the patio, so he asked her to come through the gate. He had made dinner for Amber many times before, but this time was different. *He* was different. Amber thought he seemed anxious, which was way out of character for him. Patrick was a solid dude, which was one of the things Amber found so attractive. She was drawn to his poise. He was charismatic and he was cool. But something was out of sync tonight. She couldn't put her finger on it, but tonight, something was definitely off.

After clearing their plates, Patrick called for Amber to come into the kitchen. His ruse was that he needed her to help him bring out dessert. When she walked through the French doors, Patrick was already down on one knee, surrounded by seven huge vases, each filled with a dozen red roses. The song "Ms. Grace" by The Tymes was playing softly in the background. In his hand, Patrick had an open, black velvet box. And inside the box was a two-and-a-half carat, emerald-cut diamond ring. Amber was absolutely stunned. She couldn't move. For a minute, she wasn't sure if she could even breathe. All she could do was listen to the song lyrics:

Ooo ooo ooo Miss Grace
Satin and perfume and lace
The minute I saw your face
I knew that I loved you.

Patrick had indeed proposed. He had said, "Amber Autumn Grace, will you do me the great honor of becoming my wife?" But there was no response. Finally, she heard Patrick call out to her. "Amber?" His voice, a little louder this time, caused her to snap back into reality. And through a veil of tears, Amber shouted, "Yes! Of course, I will marry you! Of course, I will!" Patrick stood up, walked over to her, and placed the ring on her finger. Then he picked her up and swung her around, just like in the movies. It had been a night like no other.

AMBER AND HER CHURCH, EAST SIDE CHURCH OF CHRIST

*E*ast Side Church of Christ typically worshipped with no music. Pastor Sullivan preferred the purity of the lyrics alone, which meant singing a cappella. They sang hymns while standing still, which was in stark contrast to the more demonstrative expressions of today's choirs and congregations. No judgment, but East Side was more about saints singing than wave-like crowd swinging.

Anna and Jake met at East Side COC when they were very young. They both attended the church's youth class held every Wednesday after school, right before prayer service. They became close friends. They hung out together. They studied together. And as they became teenagers, with hormones raging, they became even closer. So much so that they would soon discover a child had been conceived.

Little Amber was on the way, to the parentage of two

people who were really just children themselves. But God was gracious, as He always is. Amber was born healthy and happy, and while holding her accountable for her actions, Anna's family encircled her with their love, and with the love of Jesus Christ.

Jake was a typical teenage dad. He hadn't matured to any level of fatherhood. But he did visit Anna and Amber as regularly as might be reasonably expected of a teenage dad. Jake wondered to himself if he might have visited more often if Amber had been a boy. But he didn't spend too much time thinking about it. She was a girl. And besides, she had her mother, and she had her grandparents, all right there in the same house with her.

Jake justified his absence by telling himself that being around didn't make much difference. When you would rather hang out with your peers, playing Fortnite and shooting hoops, that mindset was plausible rationalization for a teenage boy.

Anna and Amber were regular attendees at East Side. Her family had forgiven her, and they continued to love and support her in her new role as a new mom. But much of the church family was less empathetic, less understanding, and frankly, less tolerant. There was even a sect of the church that had been perfectly content with Anna "taking care of" her unplanned pregnancy. She could do it discreetly, in private. No one would ever have to know.

That group viewed Anna's transgression as a reflection on East Side, and on them. They felt no compassion for a 15-

year-old girl who was young and afraid. They had no appreciation for the completely unforeseen trajectory her life was now on. Anna's mother and grandmother, much like Eunice and Lois in First Timothy, had taught her scripture. Anna knew, in spite of her sin, God had forgiven her. She knew she had the blessing of Romans 8:1, the blessing of no condemnation because she was in Christ Jesus. Still, some of the parishioners' side eyes continued to remind her of *their* condemnation.

Anna decided, for the time being, it might just be better for her to worship online. She wanted to be a part of a fellowship where forgiveness and restoration were more than bullet points on a presentation in a bible class. She wanted to find a church where forgiveness was displayed, not just talked about.

It was also important to Anna to find a church where Amber could learn and grow in God. She had been able to do that as a child, and she wanted the same for her daughter. Anna found a great church, full of children, many of them Amber's age. So Anna and Amber became members of Word Family Church.

Anna noticed Amber really liked being at church. She wanted to do everything she saw the other children doing. Amber would say to Ms. Anna, "Mommy, if they can do it, I can do it". As a child, she started out singing in the Little Angels choir. After that, she began serving as a greeter, welcoming guests and handing out visitor cards. Before long, Amber was active all over Word Family Church.

When she became a teenager, she became one of the youth speakers. Amber really enjoyed public speaking. It seemed to be intrinsic. She did it effortlessly. Little did she know that learning to speak to a church congregation was a prelude, preparing her for speaking to a judge and jury.

AMBER AND HER INNER WOMAN

*W*ith all the talk these days about being your authentic self, Amber prided herself on being blatantly honest with who she really was. She thought it wise to see herself as God saw her, looking right into the face of the good, the bad, and the ugly.

Amber was passionate about her career choice, about becoming an attorney. When she thought about righting the wrongs perpetrated in her father's case, she was fueled with determination. Yes, he was guilty. Yes, he had to pay his debt to society. But he was just a boy who was hurting after losing his older brother so tragically. He just wanted to fit in somewhere. Anywhere. After all, he was just the lookout. He didn't have a weapon. He didn't threaten anyone. To be given thirty years was *so* unfair. Amber didn't feel it was judicial.

She felt it was deliberately punitive. And she pledged to do all she could to right that wrong.

In addition to her work with the law firm, Amber periodically offered pro bono services to clients who couldn't afford representation. When she was called upon to defend some of these clients, Amber indeed felt an intimation of shame. More often than not, they looked like her. But their stories were not like her father's. Some of these clients were the masterminds of awful crimes. They would openly admit what they had done, without apology. For these particular clients, confessing was like a badge of honor. It was viewed as an initiation into some twisted boy-trying-to-be-a-man's club. But Amber had taken an oath, and agreeing to represent them bound her to the Sixth Amendment to the Constitution:

A criminal defendant's right to an attorney is found in the Sixth Amendment to the U.S. Constitution, which requires the "assistance of counsel" for the accused "in all criminal prosecutions." This means that a defendant has a constitutional right to be represented by an attorney during trial. It also means that if the defendant can't afford an attorney, in almost all instances the government will appoint one to handle the case, at no cost to the defendant.

For the clients who were arrested for lesser offenses, Amber knew they too merited the opportunity to tell their side of the story. Still, she couldn't deny that she made judgments based on their appearance. She remembered how she had been criticized, and even condemned, solely based on her looks. So she learned to look past their hair, past their tattoos, and past their sagging pants. With each case she took, even more than the sixth amendment, she kept Proverbs 18:5 ever present in her mind:

Showing partiality to the wicked is not good,
nor is depriving the innocent of justice.

To Amber, that meant no matter how much money a wicked defendant had, she couldn't show partiality. It also meant no matter how little money an innocent defendant had, he too was entitled to a defense. Even if he was found standing over the body with a bloody knife in his hand. He may indeed be guilty, but there may also be mitigating circumstances.

AMBER AND GOD HER CONFIDANT

$\mathcal{A}$mber loved her job, but her work was taxing and extremely stressful. Peoples' lives were literally in her hands. She was confident that she was good at what she did. Nobody did it better. Her skill notwithstanding, she could only control what she could control. After presenting her closing arguments, she had no way of knowing what any verdict would be. Not until she heard it announced along with everyone else in the courtroom.

Amber invested a lot of time making sure her mind and body were healthy. She was mentally sharp and physically fit. But she also knew that without devoting just as much time to the health and prosperity of her soul, the other two didn't matter much, if at all.

Amber was an early riser. She started each day at 6:00 a.m. with prayer and meditation. She had a deep love for her

God, and she was always aware that the life she was living was all about His goodness and all about His grace.

In her work, because she was a no-nonsense attorney, people outside Amber's circle rarely, if ever, saw her sensitive side. She expended a lot of energy in both the preparation and the exhibition of her court cases. As with any lawyer worth her salt, she was all in for her clients. Amber made sure the prosecution always knew she would go for the jugular in proof of her clients' innocence, especially the underprivileged she was standing up for. She was convinced she was all they had.

But in her alone time with God, Amber was free to really open up. She could just let it all out and let it all go. Those periods of time gave her the chance to focus on unrestricted worship and unabashed praise to her great God. She was free to share her heart with her Father. She was able to receive clear, in-the-moment life instructions from Him, with no distractions. The promise of His safety and security was the solid, unshakeable ground she could stand on. And of that, she was certain.

After having spent that time with Him, she was always refreshed. She was always recharged. She was always replenished. And to Amber, those were simply more of His many benefits toward her.

Let's Pause & Ponder, Let's Document & Discuss

1. How do you feel about a Christian woman wearing clothing that fully covers, yet, accentuates her body? Are there any articles of clothing that are inappropriate for a Christian woman to wear? If so, what are they? Why do you feel that way?

_____

_____

_____

_____

2. Amber was raised to celebrate who she was and to be exactly who God created her to be. In what way can walking that out be misunderstood by others? Should you respond to people who label your confidence as arrogance? If so, what does that response look like?

_____

_____

_____

_____

3. Amber grew up without her father. How does a father's absence during a child's formative years effect a child, particularly a daughter? What are some practical ways a father can establish a relationship with his adult son or daughter?

_____

_____

_____

_____

_____

4. Amber and Baileigh were great debaters. Amber was really good, as was on display when she was in the courtroom. When your viewpoint is challenged by friend or foe, how do you respond? Do you hold fast to your convictions or do you pull back? Why or why not?

_____

_____

_____

_____

_____

5. Amber knew Patrick had a reputation of being a ladies' man. Should that have been of concern to her? Why or why not? Would it be of concern to you? Why or why not?

_____

_____

_____

_____

_____

6. Ms. Anna felt driven from her church because Amber was conceived out of wedlock. How should the church family respond when a member's private sin becomes public knowledge? What are some practical ways we can show God's restorative love while simultaneously holding to God's standard?

_____

_____

_____

_____

_____

7. Being a defense attorney, Amber was sometimes required to represent questionable clients. How does she reconcile working on behalf of lawbreakers with keeping the community safe? Do you think our young men should be free from being targeted because of their hairstyles, tattoos, or sagging pants? Why or why not?

_____

_____

_____

_____

_____

8. Amber insisted on spending alone time with God. During that time, she was able to let go of all that weighed her down and stressed her out. Are you able to be completely open and honest when presenting yourself to God? Why or why not?

_____

_____

_____

_____

_____

EPILOGUE

*O*ver these past ten years, the girls hadn't communicated very much. As a matter of fact, the only time the four of them might actually get together would be if they attended the homecoming football game. Each fall, EEA would join with the students of Soaring Scholars Institute, EEA's boys' campus counterpart, to celebrate homecoming weekend. There was no particular reason why the girls hadn't connected more often, except that they were just busy. Furthering their education. Building their careers. Living their lives.

After a decade in the real world, and nearing the end of their 20s, the girls each received invites to Elevated Education Academy's ten-year class reunion. Onyx, Ven and Amber accepted right away, but Candee wasn't sure if she would attend. Her memories of her time at EEA weren't all that warm and fuzzy, so why should she have what she saw as a repeat ten years later?

Amber, ever the mediator, contacted Candee and convinced her to go. While Candee wasn't all that thrilled about spending her weekend with her high school girl group, the trip *would* give her a chance to see Mrs. Langow. She may have sometimes had her issues with the girls, be they real or illusory, Candee had to admit one thing: Mrs. Langow was always very nice to her. She never showed any bias toward any of them, and she always made sure they each knew they were important, and that they mattered.

The reunion was to be held at the Hemsworth Hotel in downtown Philly. After sharing some FaceTime and discussing the reunion with their significant others, they decided to make it a girls' weekend.

Since details were in her DNA, Ven volunteered to book a suite for their stay, beautifully adorned and complete with every amenity they could imagine. Though she would never say so, even Candee felt the excitement building.

It was a great evening. The girls had the opportunity to visit with Mrs. Langow, as well as the rest of the faculty members, and their fellow classmates. Everyone played catchup. Some exchanged email addresses. Others, phone numbers, promising to text every now and then. They all agreed to keep in touch via social media.

When the food was gone and the music was stilled, these four friends grabbed the elevator and went up to their suite. They spent the rest of the night laughing, crying, and sharing. They revealed a lot to each other about what their lives had been like over the past ten years. And they discovered they had all had similar experiences. It felt good to know that someone else could relate to many of the challenges they each had faced. What a welcome relief to know that even though they may have been walking miles apart, they hadn't been walking alone.

Whatever feelings they had about the roads their young lives had taken, they were grateful that God had put a song in each of their hearts, and that they could sing that song all along the way. God had orchestrated every note. Every soft note and every loud note. Every flat note and every sharp note. Every quiet start and every crescendo. And the one thing that made it all so wonderful was that they could look back and say, "God, You *did* that!" And we thank You!

www.ingramcontent.com/pod-product-compliance
Lightning Source LLC
LaVergne TN
LVHW011332080426
835513LV00006B/305